EDMUND BLUNDEN

EDMUND BLUNDEN

by
ALEC M. HARDIE

PUBLISHED FOR
THE BRITISH COUNCIL
BY LONGMAN GROUP LTD

LONGMAN GROUP LTD
Longman House, Burnt Mill, Harlow, Essex

*Associated companies, branches and
representatives throughout the world*

First published 1958
Revised edition 1971
© Alec M. Hardie 1958, 1971

Printed in Great Britain by
F. Mildner & Sons, London, EC1R 5EJ

SBN 0 582 01094 2

EDMUND BLUNDEN

I

EARLY in 1914 the young schoolboy, Edmund Blunden, interviewed an unworldly bookseller and printer in Horsham. His purpose was to discover the cost of publishing two slight 'volumes' of poems at his own expense. One contained translations from French poets, and the other a collection of English verses that imaged more than a schoolboy's dream of the countryside. It is to the credit of the printer that he agreed, and thought financial settlements unimportant; he may have glimpsed the young poet's later thoughts:

> How many doting eyes of poets dead
>   Have known and lost the Spirit of this sweet land
> Who to young wonder glows! and as I read,
>   Longing in past enchanted vales to stand.
>
> From pages hid away by time, or crowned
>   With timeless laurels oft on a sudden arose
> The mist of magic, and old haunted ground
>   Shone with the Spirit who to young wonder glows.

Other slim volumes followed, and it was not without significance that one was dedicated to Leigh Hunt, another to John Clare. Blunden showed an original trend of thought, now seen as very much his own, in 'The Silver Bird of Herndyke Mill'. He was richly concerned with the 'Spirit of this sweet land' and the 'mist of magic'.

His background was the countryside of Kent and Sussex. His father and mother were both from families whose roots and generations had been in the country parts of England. At the time of the birth of their eldest son, Edmund, in 1896, they were sharing the headship of a school in London, but as the family increased so did their desire to return to the country; they happened on the quiet Kentish village of Yalding, reflecting the continuity of English rural life—the gentle existence of country people going about their tasks as so many generations before them had done. Yalding was one of the few villages maintaining a Grammar School, and here Blunden received his early education. He won a scholarship to Christ's Hospital. There at Horsham he encountered the unchangeable spirit of an older England in 'the Bluecoat School'. The Tudor dress has survived, the drab breeches, yellow stockings, dark-blue cassock, broad girdle and white clerical bands. The school had a great name for giving a wide education; boys were equipped to go abroad as administrators, soldiers, or merchants, or they entered the Church, or became men of letters. Charles Lamb, a Bluecoat boy, was at once an employee of the East India Company in London and a man of letters.

Blunden inherited the intense loyalty of 'Old Blues'. Later he repaid some of his debt by writing a history of the school and in celebration of the school's fourth centenary composed the play *A Dede of Pittie*, in verse and prose, which was performed in London in 1953.

He became a member of the House named after Coleridge, and the first book he bought for himself was Coleridge's poems. So began a lifelong study of other Old Blues; among them Leigh Hunt; and Shelley associations with the school estate attracted the boy. Not least of Christ's Hospital's demands was good handwriting; to admire the strong and sensitive Blunden script is to recollect that the school was among the last to have writing-masters, and that throughout its history boys have gone there to learn the copperplate familiar in the books of London's great business houses.

His career at school went well; he became senior 'Grecian', won prizes for Greek and Latin verses, experimented in translating the classics and French into English. The experiment has become part of his art; few translators now have the classical grounding and the poet's care shown in Blunden's translations of the Latin poems of Marvell and Milton.

No one was surprised when he gained the senior classics scholarship at The Queen's College, Oxford.

II

But the year was 1914. Some months later he joined the Royal Sussex Regiment and was thrown into the life of an army training camp, a fierce peripety for a young man who had been sheltered in the security of his native countryside and the continuity of an ancient school. The effect of the years of war on his nervous sensitivity he has told himself in *Undertones of War*, the echoes of which continue.

He wisely did not attempt to make that record until years after, in 1928, when artistic detachment had guided his emotions. It is the outstanding example of an author creating in retrospect the moment of human waste, emphasizing war as man's greatest error, not by uncontrolled savage shocks and crudities, but by quietness, restraint, by understatement.

Something more is needed to explain why this true personal statement should remain equally significant after another war and rumours of war. Artistically it is an integrated work that avoids the episodic; instead, it flows along in a quick stream of continuous and connected thought in which the prose-writer is identified with the poet. But that would be insufficient to indicate why in Britain *Undertones of War* has appeared in many editions, or why a popular edition was published in Japan in 1956.

Perhaps one of the most reasoned prophetic considerations of *Undertones of War* was given by H. M. Tomlinson[1] in

---

[1] 'War Books', by H. M. Tomlinson, *The Criterion*, April 1930.

1930. After reflecting upon several other war records, Tomlinson declared:

As you read deeply . . . your uneasiness grows. This poet's eye is not in a fine frenzy rolling. There is a steely glitter in it . . . Blunden's book, in fact, is by a ghost for other ghosts; some readers will not know what it is all about . . . Yet it is a humorous book, though its fun is wan; through pale fun you can see the tangibilities of today solid in their appropriate places . . . His cheerful voice is addressed over your shoulder, and your amusement fades when that fancy chills it. You turn round; and nothing is there!

This 'uneasiness' is more than the 'atmosphere' of the book; it is Blunden's method of disturbing his readers into understanding his undertones. Tomlinson continues:

The men are the best of Blunden's book; and that is right. That at least we were sure to get from a poet. This story of war stirs and proceeds with living figures, and its scenes are authentic . . . Something aeolian breathes through its lines. You may hear echoing, as one used to hear desolation murmuring when the night was suspect and the flares above the trenches were few before dawn, the wonder and awe of the sacrificed who did not know why this had come to them; for Blunden's is a tribute to the unknown soldier more lasting than the pomps about a cenotaph.

It is the ghost of the 'unknown soldier' that makes the whole narrative universal and exact. The author tries to stay in the background; the reader hears comparatively little of his own reactions. His comrades, in the strong bond which can link strangers together under uncertainties and dangers, are the central figures, figures of humanity split by an unknown force into allies and foes. The very 'uneasiness' and the friendships are symbols of the poet trying to depict allies and foes together in the name of man; of so dramatizing common feelings that horror and revulsion result. The moments before the opening of a battle were opportunities for eeriness, instinctive fear and strange humour, as at the Battle of the Somme:

Another postponement took me dustily back to the battalion in the
wood watched by so many German observation-balloons in the morning
sun. The wood, shelled deliberately because of its camps and accidentally
because of some conspicuous horse-lines and silhouetted movements on
the hill to the west, had frayed the men's keenness; there had been
casualties; and then the anticlimax twice repeated had spoiled their first
energetic eagerness for a battle. Yet, still, they were a sound and capable
battalion, deserving far better treatment than they were now getting,
and a battle, not a massacre. On the evening of September 2, the
battalion moved cautiously from Mailly-Maillet by cross-country
tracks, through pretty Englebelmer, with ghostly Angelus on the green
and dewy light, over the downs to Mesnil, and assembled in the Hamel
trenches to attack the Beaucourt ridge next morning. The night all
round was drugged and quiet. I stood at the junction of four advanced
trenches, directing the several companies into them as had been planned.
Not one man in thirty had seen the line by daylight—and it was a maze
even when seen so, map in hand. Even climbing out of the narrow steep
trenches with weighty equipment, and crossing others by bridges placed
'near enough' in this dark last moment, threatened to disorder the
assault. Every man remembered the practice attacks at Monchy-Breton,
and was ready, if conditions were equal, to act his part; among other
things, the 'waves' had to form up and carry out a 'right incline' in No
Man's Land—a change of direction almost impossible in the dusk, in
broken and entangled ground, and under concentrated gunfire. When
the rum and coffee were duly on the way to these men, I went off to my
other duty. A carrying-party from another battalion was to meet me in
Hamel, and for a time the officer and I, having nothing to do but wait,
sat in a trench beside the village high street considering the stars in their
courses. An unusual yet known voice jubilantly interrupted this unnaturally calm conversation; it was a sergeant-major, a fine soldier who
had lost his rank for drunkenness, won it again, and was now going over
in charge of a party carrying trench-mortar ammunition. A merry man,
a strong man; when we had met before, he had gained my friendliest
feelings by his freedom from any feeling against a school-boy officer.
Some NCOs took care to let their superior training and general wisdom
weigh on my shyness: not so C. He referred to the attack as one might
speak of catching a train, and in it a few hours later he showed such
wonderful Saint Christopher spirit that he was expected to be awarded
a posthumous Victoria Cross. Meanwhile all waited.

The poems written during the war in the same spirit

reveal the swift maturity, only half-comprehended, which
war forces upon youth. Through *Undertones of War* the
soldier seizing every moment to be a poet is clear enough.
Equally clear—and significant—is his awareness of the
French and Belgian countryside. He may long for Sussex,
but the rivers and lanes of Flanders hold the same fascination
for him:

> Now bitter frosts, muffling the morn
> In old days, crunch the grass anew;
> There where the floods made fields forlorn
> The glinzy ice grows thicker through.
> The pollards glower like mummies when
> Thieves break into a pyramid,
> Inscrutable as those dead men
> With painted mask and balm-cloth hid.

His irony is rarely cynical, his anger rarely outrageous.
The memory of his youth is mingled with the horror of his
experience; a flower takes on a new meaning when set
beside a gun; and he feels bewildered, as when preparations
are being made for an attack:

> Days or eternities like swelling waves
> Surge on, and still we drudge in this dark maze.
> The bombs and coils and cans by strings of slaves
> Are borne to serve the coming day of days;
> Pale sleep in slimy cellars scarce allays
> With its brief blank the burden. Look, we lose;
> The sky is gone, the lightless drenching haze
> Of rainstorm chills the bones; earth, air are foes,
> The black fiend leaps brick-red as life's last picture goes.

It was after his discharge in 1919 that the real impact
slowly and insidiously made itself felt. The world, and
England in particular, had irrevocably changed. For older
men more experienced and saddened by life the return to
peace was not easy; for one so young and sensitive the
imprint of the experience could not be eradicated, and was
almost the standard by which the rest of life was to be

judged. With many others he joined in trying to explain
his disillusionment, not with self-pity but with an urgent
desire to prevent another such disaster to the dignity of
man. In such sympathy and with a poet's care he helped to
introduce Wilfred Owen's poems to the world. After
Kipling's death Blunden added his voice to the Imperial
War Graves Commission.

The ghosts have never left him, and, as with so many of
his generation, have haunted him ever since:

> The struggling Ancre had no part
>   In these new hours of mine,
> And yet its stream ran through my heart;
>   I heard it grieve and pine,
> As if its rainy tortured blood
>   Had swirled into my own,
> When by its battered bank I stood
>   And shared its wounded moan.

Such memories have shaped his mind to the purpose of
life, and even appear as he paints his own countryside. If
Sussex were to be found in France, France he sees no less
in Wiltshire:

> My feet, along this road, above that stream,
>   Drop into marching time,
>   Make wild arithmetic of time—
> So like this valley and that dead one seem.

It is not strange that he feels a great affection for peaceful
France and the French way of life, equal to his appreciation
of French literature.

III

A civilian with military decorations, a man who had been
a boy when last out of uniform, he decided to take up his
Scholarship and return to Oxford. More important than

studying for classical honours, however, was the task of
coming to terms with himself. He recorded, soon after, the
dilemma of this personal aftermath:

> The eyes that had been strength so long
> Gone, or blind, or lapt in clay,
> And war grown twenty times as strong
> As when I held him first at bay;
>
> Then down and down I sunk from joy
> To shrivelled age, though scarce a boy,
> And knew for all my fear to die
> That I with those lost friends should lie.

He presently surmised that Oxford was not for him;
it was hardly likely that undergraduate life would be
sympathetic to prematurely 'shrivelled age'. Restless, he
moved out of College to a small cottage on Boar's Hill,
where many of the young literary group often made their
way. Oxford had again become a 'nest of singing birds';
among the voices heard were those of Robert Graves,
Robert Nichols, Edgell Rickword, Alan Porter, William
Force Stead, Louis Golding and L. A. G. Strong. Garsington
Manor was thriving under Lady Ottoline Morrell. She
welcomed young writers who might meet John Middleton
Murry, Katherine Mansfield, Mark Gertler, Desmond
MacCarthy, Augustine Birrell, Henry Lamb, the promising
novelist Aldous Huxley.

Not long before going back to the University he sent his
early poems 'for the favour of review' to Siegfried Sassoon,
the literary editor of the new *Daily Herald*. During the war
he had never stopped writing and reading. Apologizing for
this diversion he excused himself for having to eat even in
the trenches. Sassoon now saw 'The Barn', a poem that
contained much 'mist of magic':

> The barn is old, and very old,
> But not a place of spectral fear.
> Cobwebs and dust and speckling sun

Come to old buildings every one.
Long since they made their dwelling here,
    And here you may behold

Nothing but simple wane and change;
Your tread will wake no ghost, your voice
Will fall on silence undeterred.
No phantom wailing will be heard,
Only the farm's blithe cheerful noise.
    The barn is old, not strange.

Sassoon saw the value of the poems, asked the author
to go to London, and for the occasion collected at 39 Half
Moon Street, Edward Shanks, W. J. Turner and J. C.
Squire. It was an important meeting for the newly displayed
poet, and Sassoon and Squire became two of his greatest
friends.

In the London of 1919 many had a happy belief in literature; whatever else might change in post-war England
literature and the arts would always be needed, always
encouraged. Many tried hard to do their part in fostering
talent. Their zest and their experience delighted Blunden;
when offered the opportunity, he quitted Oxford for
London literary life. In 1920 he joined *The Athenæum*
magazine as assistant to his schoolfellow, Middleton Murry.
The beliefs that such men held were hardly shared by the
general public; in 1921 *The Athenæum* was amalgamated
with *The Nation* under the illustrious editorship of H. W.
Massingham. Blunden remained as a regular contributor.

IV

While he was still at Oxford Blunden was able to expand
his knowledge, and deepen his early appreciation, of John
Clare, the poet from Northamptonshire, friend of Charles
Lamb and other writers in the old *London Magazine*. With
his friend Alan Porter he spent much time, that Homer
might have claimed, in Peterborough carefully going

through manuscripts, and persuading Clare's descendants to produce more; he enlisted the help of the poet's grandson. This research was the first of many, and it was a considerable undertaking for a young man. He was thereby responsible for rediscovering Clare and arousing a new understanding and assessment on which all later interpreters have relied.

Both his long reading of Clare and his innate poetical appreciation of country words, expressions and metres helped him greatly to establish the most likely text in the welter of variations. So too his penetration into the connexion of man and poet is shrewd and affectionate:

The poetry of John Clare, originally simple description of the country and countrymen, or ungainly imitation of the poetic tradition as he knew it through Allan Ramsay, Burns, and the popular writers of the eighteenth century, developed into a capacity for exact and complete nature-poetry and for self-expression. Thoroughly awake to all the finest influences in life and in literature, he devoted himself to poetry in every way. Imagination, colour, melody and affection were his by nature; where he lacked was in dramatic impulse and in passion, and sometimes his incredible facility in verse, which enabled him to complete poem after poem without pause or verbal difficulty, was not his best friend. He possesses a technique of his own; his rhymes are based in pronunciation to which his ear had been trained, and thus he accurately joins 'stoop' and 'up', or 'horse' and 'cross'—while his sonnets are free and often unique in form. In spite of his individual manner, there is no poet who in his nature-poetry so completely subdues self and mood and deals with the topic for its own sake. That he is by no means enslaved to nature-poetry, the variety of the poems in this selection must show.

His Asylum Poems are distinct from most of the earlier work. They are often the expression of his love tragedy, yet strange to say they are not often sad or bitter: imagination conquers, and the tragedy vanishes. They are rhythmically new, the movement having changed from that of quiet reflection to one of lyrical enthusiasm: even nature is now seen in brighter colours and sung in subtler music. Old age bringing ever intenser recollection and childlike vision found Clare writing the light lovely songs which bear no slightest sign of the cruel years. So near in these later poems are sorrow and joy that they awaken deeper feelings and instincts than almost any other lyrics can—emotions such as he shares with us in his 'Adieu!'

> I left the little birds
> And sweet lowing of the herds,
> And couldn't find out words,
>   Do you see,
> To say to them good-bye,
> Where the yellowcups do lie;
> So heaving a deep sigh,
>   Took to sea . . .

In this sort of pathos, so indefinable and intimate, William Blake and only he can be said to resemble him.

V

Meanwhile, as Blunden was proving himself a masterly writer of reviews and essays for periodicals, able to condense in one short paragraph a wealth of understanding and appreciation, he devoted his poetic energy to the manners and scenes of English country life. His youth, background, education and experience had all prepared him for this moment, and the volumes that appeared during the war of 1914-18 had strengthened his technical mastery and perception. Throughout the years in the trenches he had carried a volume of Edward Young's *Night Thoughts*, and John Clare's poems were usually with him. Thomson's *The Seasons* and de la Mare's works were often handled. Now to his knowledge of Kent and Sussex countryside he added the very different landscape of Suffolk, where he spent his leisure hours.

During these early post-war years his reputation and fame rapidly grew as the volume of *The Waggoner* (1920) was succeeded by *The Shepherd* (1922), which brought him the Hawthornden Prize. He had a great descriptive power which allowed him to develop his individual rural poetry, but he was never just the 'pastoral' poet; he knew too well the harshness of country life. He was not didactic or moralizing; 'He approaches Reality by another, the artist's road'. Few have looked so closely and found so much in the minutest detail; he not only delighted in words and their music but he brought a sharpness to small moments that easily escape the less watchful:

> Now the old hedger with his half-moon-hook,
> Plashing the spiked thorn, musing of bygone men,
> Shakes the crab-apples plopping in the brook
> Till jangling wildgeese flush from the drowned fen—
> Nodding he plods in his gray revery,
> Self-sorry robins humouring his thoughts cast;
> While scarce perceived, by red walls warm with peaches,
>   By bosque and signal-tree,
> And otters'-lodges on the river-reaches,
> The feather-footed moments tiptoe past.

He was writing from too full an experience and too practical a knowledge to fall into the trap of sentimentality. He turns to a humour, not droll but briefly spoken as by a countryman himself. In the 'Mole Catcher' by simple art he heightens the character of the trapper:

> And moles to him are only moles; but hares
> See him afield and scarcely cease to nip
> Their dinners, for he harms not them; he spares
> The drowning fly that of his ale would sip.

Here is the sturdiness of an Uncle Toby.

One line will hint the sly humour, as in 'Forefathers' he describes the long generations of the unknown, the unread countrymen, and in the last line of the stanza sharply brings the reader back to the extent of their worth:

> Names are vanished, save the few
>   In the old brown Bible scrawled;
> These were men of pith and thew,
>   Whom the city never called;
> Scarce could read, or hold a quill,
> Built the barn, the forge, the mill.

In most of these poems lingers a sense of the sorrow that a keen contemplation of Nature indulges; a vivid melancholy mixed with wonder and mystery. 'The Pike', by the very freedom of its construction, hints at more than a river scene, but the reader is hardly prepared for the shock of the final stanza:

> Sudden the gray pike changes, and quivering
> > poises for slaughter.
> Intense terror wakens around him, the shoals
> > scud awry, but there chances
> A chub unsuspecting; the prowling fins quicken,
> > in fury he lances;
> And the miller that opens the hatch stands amazed
> > at the whirl in the water.

The complete beauty of 'Almswomen', with its strong pathos, changes its tone from the brightness of a summer's day to the fearfulness of loneliness at night. When the world is well we can forget 'Death's shadow at the door', but in darkness we have to face ourselves:

> But when those hours wane
> Indoors they ponder, scared by the harsh storm
> Whose pelting saracens on the window swarm,
> And listen for the mail to clatter past
> And church clock's deep bay withering on the blast;
> They feed the fire that flings its freakish light
> On pictured kings and queens grotesquely bright.

'The Shepherd' with its delineations echoes a similar sense of foreboding, timelessness, the curious reality of all nature:

> The hounded leaf has found a tongue to warn
> How fierce the fang of winter, the lead rain
> Brings him old pictures of the drowning plain,
> When even his dog sulks loath to face the morn.
> The sun drops cold in a water cloud, the briars
> Like starved arms still snatch at his withered fires.

In 'The Waggoner' the mysterious is again accentuated,
not with whimsy, but with a more shivering wonderment:

> The odd light flares on shadows vast

> Over the lodges and oasts and byres
> Of the darkened farm; the moment hangs wan
> As though nature flagged and all desires,
> But in the dim court the ghost is gone

> From the hug-secret yew to the penthouse wall
>   And stooping there seems to listen to
> The waggoner leading the gray to stall,
>   As centuries past itself would do.

Blunden followed no school or fashion. The post-war
disillusion hit hard at the literary world, old gods apparently
had feet of clay, and newness, originality and revolt were
the catchwords. To believe in the immediate past was to
believe in sterility and decadence. Edmund Blunden was
labelled a 'Georgian' by many of the rebels, and that term
was taken to unify a group of poets quite diverse in age,
temperament, environment and writing, who frequently
had not even met each other.

Very early in his career it was seen that his mastery of
language, imagery and technique was unusually strong.
He enjoyed words and found music in the conversation of
the countryman. He lingered over their possibilities, and
added a virility to many of his verses by the skilful use of
dialect. Robert Bridges was among the first to realize this
art and after the publication of *The Waggoner* in 1920 wrote
a detailed analysis of the dialectal diction in the poems:

Since a young poet, Mr Edmund Blunden, has lately published a
volume in which this particular element of dialectal and obsolescent
words is very prominent, it will be suitable to our general purpose to
consider it as a practical experiment and examine the results. The poetic
diction and high standard of his best work give sufficient importance to
this procedure; and though he may seem to be somewhat extravagant
in his predilection for unusual terms, yet his poetry cannot be imagined
without them.

His country poetry continued to increase his reputation, and as he experimented widely in ballads, lyrics, songs and love poems a more profound note was struck. The effect of the war would not allow him to pursue any other course; through his mind the themes were mixed—war, waste, nature, man's experience and man's relation to God. He struggled to connect all he knew, rather than give way to bitterness, a despairing negative creed. His imagination, more delicately poised over reality, went with a haunting dream-like quality. In 'The Midnight Skaters', for example, who are these figures, and what is the pond on which they move? Here, as so often, by the delicacy of the imagery he heightens his effect, and in the last verse the rhythm moves rapidly, eerily, and with the simplest language:

> The hop-poles stand in cones,
>   The icy pond lurks under,
> The pole-tops steeple to the thrones
>   Of stars, sound gulfs of wonder;
> But not the tallest there, 'tis said,
> Could fathom to this pond's black bed.
>
> Then is not death at watch
>   Within those secret waters?
> What wants he but to catch
>   Earth's heedless sons and daughters?
> With but a crystal parapet
> Between, he has his engines set.
>
> Then on, blood shouts, on, on,
>   Twirl, wheel and whip above him,
> Dance on this ball-floor thin and wan,
>   Use him as though you love him;
> Court him, elude him, reel and pass,
> And let him hate you through the glass.

Water, streams and rivers have always fascinated him. Earlier, life had been a gentle flowing stream, attractively clear and shallow, but now the stream had turned into a river with unknown depths that were hazardous and yet had to be explored. He looks again at one of his boyhood streams, and writes:

> And do you then, gentle stream,
> Assume your wintriest wild extreme,
> And (as I have known amazed) pour down
> Among your goblin willows brown
> Deep-dooming floods and foaming flocks
> Of whirlwaves till the midnight rocks
> With what you say to those who dare
> Affront you with some coarse affair.

From his own 'wintriest wild extreme' he was given some relief. His health had never been good since the war, and in the hope of making a recovery he crossed to South America in a cargo boat, and the travel-book *The Bonadventure* was the result, a volume that showed a man of letters with a keen awareness of new experiences. It was the evidence of imaginative travelling much farther than from Sussex to Flanders.

VI

Soon after his journey to South America a suggestion was made by his friend Ralph Hodgson that seemed unlikely and impossible; it was that he should go to Japan for a period. Hodgson was himself about to go to Tohoku University. Blunden hesitated, but when Professor Takeshi Saito made a direct personal request, he agreed, and so became Professor of English Literature at Tokyo University for three years.

Few could then forecast the immense impact he would have on the people of Japan as a scholar, poet and man. Quite unconsciously he brought a sympathy and toleration that allowed him to make friends quickly with a people shy and easily rebuffed; they found his sincerity easy to trust. As a scholar his knowledge of English Literature had been acquired not through the grim syllabus set for a university degree, but because he enjoyed reading and literature as part of his way of living. The Japanese were waiting for such enthusiasm; they had the unbounded curiosity of students wanting to learn, to know all that was good in English. In three years Blunden augmented a tradition that Lafcadio Hearn had started. He rather created a new one, and that Japan's standard of English scholarship is so high and Japanese students so alive to its possibilities must go greatly to the credit of Edmund Blunden. 'You loved imagination's commonwealth'—many eminent and internationally known scholars and professors support this claim, all proudly acknowledging themselves Blunden's ex-pupils.

Anyone who goes on a mission to another country undertakes severe responsibilities; he has to understand and respect the name, customs and traditions of that people before he can begin to hint at the best of his own. He must know the virtues before he censures the faults. The poet who found a bond between Belgium and Wiltshire, between Sussex and France instinctively found that, with all the great differences of another civilization, there was beneath a common essence:

> We moved . . .
> Into a most familiar air,
> And like spring showers received it from the hills
> That stood from our old hills ten thousand miles—
> Or none; we paused along the yellow plains
> And kissed the child that ran from shyer friends
> To take our hand.

He pays poetical tribute to the Japanese scene, and respects it with a modesty that is his main quality as man and poet. His gentle courtesy appears in 'The Author's Last Words to his Students':

> For even the glories that I most revered,
>   Seen through a gloomed perspective in strange mood,

Were not what to our British seers appeared;
  I spoke of peace, I made a solitude,
Herding with deathless graces
My hobbling commonplaces.

Forgive that eyeless lethargy which chilled
  Your ardours and I fear dimmed much fine gold—
What your bright passion, leaping ages, thrilled
  To find and claim, and I yet dared withhold;
These and all chance offences
Against your finer senses.

To the Japanese whose traditions are in quietness, courtesy
and modesty, Blunden was no enigma. He kept his connexion when he left the country; he wrote after that for
their periodicals and books. Quite a number of volumes
published in Japan for Japanese readers portray Blunden's
devotion to the spirit of the East.

Many years later in 1947 with his wife and family he
returned to Tokyo as cultural Liaison Officer to the British
Mission. He lectured for two years in nearly every university
in the country, often to very large audiences. He was
received by prefects and governors as an official guest and
entertained accordingly.

Edmund Blunden is a living legend in Japan, and his
reception in 1947 was proof that the Japanese are full
of admiration for things English, and that they can see the
two countries linked in the serenity of this poet's vision.

No one who has been in Japan for even a short time can
fail to be impressed by the personal affection and genuine
respect that his name inspires. It transcends trivialities and
attains the dignity of a moral embassy. As the well-known
Japanese novelist Tomoji Abe recently noted: 'He is
Japan's best friend: he brings out the best in us.'

Apart from this judgement the country paid him its
highest honour in 1950 when he was elected a member of
the Japan Academy (Professor Einstein was elected at the
same time), an honour rarely accorded to a foreigner and
then usually to the great names of Science.

VII

In 1928 Blunden returned to England and to the office of *The Nation*. He was able also to return to Kent and to live at Yalding in the rambling Elizabethan house, Cleave's, that he had admired since childhood when it was the home of his Grammar School master. An interim followed while he resumed old ties and settled some of his questionings. By writing *Undertones of War* in Japan he had rid himself of many of his haunting fears.

It was almost inevitable that he should be needed by Oxford again, and he was elected a Fellow and Tutor of Merton College in 1931.

It was a prudent election, for since his work on Clare he had become a true example of the scholar-poet. From schooldays books have been his main occupation. Book-collecting is a most pleasurable labour; in the back-streets of strange towns or on the barrows of the Farringdon Road he has made unexpected discoveries. What is more important, he uses his books; it has been said of him 'he buys a book, he reads it, he then knows it'. Even more unexpected is his ability to know the detailed background of the most unknown writer. His poems often reflect his enthusiasm for newly found authors; he never deliberately quotes from another, but he possesses the well-read poet's ability so to absorb the spirit of others that we discern his recent reading of Thomson, Vaughan, Young, Chatterton, the Wartons.

As a scholar he is always the poet—and so the man; a poet who enjoys words and language, a man who imagines the blood and thought of the author's mind. 'One short essay by Blunden will tell more of King Lear than a whole volume by others.' He can very simply drive through a mist of critical irrelevancies and reach the essence of the mind behind the work. In 'The Age of Herbert and Vaughan', for example, he sums up much in short quick stanzas:

And where young Prue was sweeping,
　　Or giggling at the gate,
Or Tom was scaring crows
　　Or the dog Sam licked the plate
Or ewe and lamp were sleeping,

The witness still recorded
　　Glance, phrase and incident
That appertained to Christ
　　And by these shows was meant.
At once he stood rewarded.

Brief essays, like those on Vaughan, Traherne, George
Herbert, express his sensitive judgement and penetration.
His edition of William Collins and the essay there in introduction combine the facts of biography with a delicacy of
thought that is appropriate to the slight figure of the author
of 'The Passions'. Blunden has followed his own way in
biography and criticism, as in poetry, and it is a way that
restores the word criticism to its proper and fuller meaning,
that of judgement or estimation rather than condemnation.
It is easier to apply external rules to a work than to discover
the mind of the author. He is temperamentally unwilling
to show other than sympathy; he makes a real attempt to
meet an author on his own level, to know what he is trying
to say, and not to force prejudices upon a victim.

Rightly he has the reputation of a kindly critic, preferring
to find the author's qualities and to gloss over faults. But it
would be a great mistake to believe him innocent or in-
discriminate; because he takes so much trouble his principles
are correspondingly high, and his judgements are graded
according to the quality of the work before him. His
methods, with his understanding and love of words and
language, allow him to discover the bogus and the in-
sincere. He is never the popular dictator of values; he writes
and judges with care, every word is chosen with subtle
shrewdness, and sometimes the sting is not immediately felt.

As a critic he demands the return of the compliment that
he pays; if he takes care, he requires that of the reader.

Above all, his sensitivity and scholarship have made him one of the leading authorities on the Romantic poets and writers. He expanded his early interest in Leigh Hunt and formed a fresh living interpretation. His full-length study shows a sympathetic understanding of the man, and gives him a considerable position as a man of his period. He even rescued the gentle Kirke White from the dusty corner of the bookshops.

Wordsworth, Keats, Shelley and their friends have claimed much of his attention. A full biography of Shelley by Blunden had long been overdue when it appeared in 1946, and as a composition in prose this volume ranks with *Undertones of War*. It is equally a major contribution to Shelleyan scholarship. The ethereal myth and bloodless unreality surrounding Shelley in the past were scattered, and instead he was portrayed as the poet and man of intellect, science and vision.

On the first page of this biography Blunden lays down the idea of the subject:

Genius, time and reputation have done their work; and it has been often felt or concluded that Shelley, as if by some inexplicable chance or caprice of nature, sprang in his single greatness out of a family which apart from him continued through the centuries without distinction, energy or noble error. Undoubtedly the way in which Shelley lived and the nature of his vision of gods and men would have perplexed all or almost all his ancestors, just as the new style in which he wrote English poetry would have astonished such of them as had some acquaintance with its standard examples. On closer view he appears not utterly isolated from all those others. Here and there some touch of them survives in him to make us aware that the poet was of their breed, and to limit if not to overcome the supposition that except for him there is little colour in the annals of the Shelleys. To what extent the scientist of heredity is able to see him deriving from them is a question beyond my range, yet characteristics of theirs, unless we yield all to coincidence, make it desirable to approach him through some of the Shelleys before him. A glance at the fragmentary records is justified moreover because Shelley himself was perfectly well aware, in no spirit of vanity, that he belonged to an ancient house; because he grew up amidst its relics and in responsibility to the local world which it had shaped; because indeed but for its stored-up power and fortune he could not have led the life that he did. Even his endeavours in the cause of the less fortunate part of society, his contributions to an overthrow of the old order, inevitably rested upon that order and had the mark of the aristocrat, much as we find with Tolstoi.

His critical range is wide, from Shakespeare to George Darley, from Christopher Smart to Hardy, from Chatterton to Wilfred Owen. There are probably two general qualities in his interest in all English literature, sincerity of purpose and a call for sympathy. Nearly every author whom he examines has not only something of the purely poetic about him, a spark of visionary fire, but some personal reason for deserving sympathy as a man; prolonged ill-health, madness, suicide, or some inability to deal with the circumstances of his time.

VIII

By the time he returned to Oxford a calmer and quieter mood pervaded his work. A more certain note of belief is evident; 'Report on Experience' tells something:

> Say what you will, our God sees how they run.
> These disillusions are his curious proving
> That he loves humanity and will go on loving;
> Over there are faith, life, virtue in the sun.

These lines were not the end but the beginning of a deeper searching into the relationship between nature, 'the mysterious Mother', and the human and spiritual mind. In 'Values' he asks himself and his reader to combine intellect and emotion and find the basic essence of man, using language and imagery that are Shakespearian in their tensity and vastness:

Till darkness lays a hand on these gray eyes
And out of man my ghost is sent alone,
It is my chance to know that force and size
Are nothing but by answered undertone,
No beauty even of absolute perfection
Dominates here—the glance, the pause, the guess
Must be my amulets of resurrection;
Raindrops may murder, lightnings may caress.

There I was tortured, but I cannot grieve;
There crowned and palaced—visibles deceive.
That storm of belfried cities in my mind
Leave me my vespers cool and eglantined.
From love's wide-flowering mountain-side I chose
This spring of green, in which an angel shows.

An awesome note alternates with his peace, more intense than many acclaimed voices of the mystical. Throughout the thirties he wrote in this way, and as his works were more highly metaphysical, he exercised more emotional control over the undercurrent. These were years in which the very climate of the world—and he had never shut out the world—made the task more than usually difficult.

Over much of his work of the period lingers the academic atmosphere of Oxford; the number of set literary pieces, of verses addressed to past authors and unknown divines, together with the humour of such as 'Incident in Hyde Park 1803', increases. Lyrics and ballads, sketches from the country are mingled with more memories of the war. Often he permits himself to grow angry, as the years bring nearer a repetition of what he hoped, standing apart from politics and full of mankind's faith, could never happen again. 'Exorcised' is Blunden at his fiercest:

Twenty years had nearly passed, and while these watched
    they saw aghast
That giant enemy of sleep, that ghost which summed the
    worst they knew,
Come creeping into waking thought, creeping and gathering
    like a storm

About the summer's loveliness, a vaster, more inhuman
    form.
        The dream was coming true.

Back to your madhouse, child of hell: too many of us
    know you well;
Infest our sleep, if thence we keep some record of your
    eyeless eyes,
But trespass not in the face of day. You find you cannot
    prowl this way;
Your very foulness forearmed those who now have
    checked your matinée,
        The generous, selfless, wise.

It was as though some foreboding allowed him no peace;
this was the one period where often his works contain many
'half-ideas, verges of shadows and misty brightness'. In
many diverse pieces he asserts, defiantly, 'calm in calm
atmosphere', or how 'the safe paths curve through unexalted
fields'. He writes anxiously, and in his best moments the
searching emotional tone makes his readers think carefully.
Oddly, it was in 1940, just after the war began, that he freed
himself and, as though his personal and intellectual ideas
were clarified, wrote 'The Sum of All':

Crossing the artillery ranges whose fierce signs
Mean nothing now; whose gougings look like
Bird-baths now; and last, the frontier farm
And guard-house made of bracken.
Rising to this old eyrie, quietly forsaken,
You bear me on, and not me only.
All difference sheds away,
All shrivelling of the sense, anxious prolepsis,
Injury, staring suspicion,
Fades into pure and wide advance.
So rise; so let me pass.

IX

His fears and anxiety had been concentrated on hoping that
the disaster of another world war would be prevented,

but once it happened, he could not persist in backward lamentations. He retained the poet's vision that this second outbreak would be more devastating; the power of destruction had become so much greater and the ability to control the machine correspondingly weaker. However, basically he reasserted his confidence in the faith of the past, that the best spirit of man, almost the divine spark of man, would survive:

> Men have that in them which desires the flower,
> The perfume and the music of their age,
> That governs them, that glorifies the hour
> When, severally resolved, their hosts engage
> In indescribable battle . . .
> The generous strength which out of depth and din
> Has lifted men to escurials is not dead.

Once again he put on uniform and found himself instructing among others some of the young war poets, until he left Oxford in 1943. He returned to a war-scarred London and joined the staff of *The Times Literary Supplement*. Despite the war these were active years when his studies of Thomas Hardy and Shelley were written. And he paid his tribute to his favourite sport that had started in boyhood at Yalding, cricket. He is the first poet to write verses for a Test Match captain! *Cricket Country* was not only an affectionate book reflecting the game, it was a timely affirmation that the philosophy of cricket would outlast temporary setbacks. Philip Tomlinson likened it in its sphere to Walton's *Compleat Angler* as it roams in gentle and reminiscent thought over the game and the world around.

As a poet Blunden began what may be considered his third period. Such divisions are arbitrary and often misleading, but the two volumes, *Shells by a Stream* and *After the Bombing*, published between 1940 and 1950, offer a change of mind and technique. His voice became, as though to counter the confusion of the period, more distinct; its simplicity was still subtlety, because the thought was increasingly metaphysical as the language grew less involved.

Sometimes he suggests that he is not quite the source of this confident note:

> It is not mine to choose; the deeper call
> Is master yet. The child is that they made him.

And though death is brought nearer to the world, yet, because of that, life has a lighter, subtly happier cause:

> O living love in whose great birth
> Death counts for nothing, proved a lie,
> Still blaze and blossom through old earth,
> And sea and sky.

Any imaginative poet, such as Blunden, justifies the theory of 'unacknowledged legislator', not in the simple sense of the term but in the ability to foresee the temper of the future; he pierces the coming mind of man, and is always some years ahead of the moment of writing. Many of his poems written in the thirties gave warning of the trials of war, the poems written during or just after the war went further forward beyond the years:

> The splendours of the world
> Are such that number and inquiring fade;
> There is no reason for them but themselves,
> That they are such, is felt as wonderful
> Compared with what they grow from; so it is.

Hope and security can come to man through a plain faith of understanding the pattern of creation, and he avers it with delicate imagery in 'The Blueprint'

> Will you too fashion a church that's awake to the April
>   showers
> Where the merry angels are ready to wing
> In the painted roof with praise and prayer
> To one who being heaven's King
> Is splendour enthroned over earth's dim air?
> A church where the altar lilies appear as the soul's new
>   flowers?

The range is as wide as ever; memories of the countryside are clearer, and the light notes as 'The Blackthorn Bush in Spring' are more simply lyrical. One of the clearest poems of this kind is a tribute to his wife, 'Serena', in which the calmness of his mind is reflected in the language:

> And yet I bless besides caprice
> That heavenly quietude, my dear,
> That pure serene, that lulling peace
> Which knows no haste, and dreams no fear,
> Like evening skies in countries where
> Great belfries shine in golden air.
>
> This peace that looks from your wide eyes
> And on your lip rests, even your hand,
> Is such an earthly paradise
> That I delighted understand
> What life could be for humankind
> Were peace so pictured to their mind.

Of considerable poetical importance were his thoughts on time, change, ghosts and God which had been a source of power for him since his early days. They were all inter-linked, and the first war, and the ways of the countryside had played a part in this interest and speculation. The years had intensified his preoccupation and now, as with his other subjects, a purity of inspiration is frequently apparent:

> We speak of ghosts, as those who from some fold
> Of death escape, and as cold shades flit by
> We ponder change, watch in our lifetime die
> A multitude of scenes; yet some will hold
> These terms of time, ghost, change and death unmeaning
> Compared with that deep presence of all in one
> Which through our common notions intervening
> Adds magic to the moonlight, gives the sun
> Another glory; and quiet place and day
> Disclose for a flash the boundless, timeless play.

Several poems dealing with timelessness and ghosts stand out, but two are great achievements, and have the simplicity of the mysterious tale where reality and imagination touch only to fly apart again. The two poems are 'When the Statue Fell' and 'Thomasine'. The former tells of the Statue of the Virgin and Child on a church-tower in Picardy. The church was almost totally destroyed; the statue remained:

> The Queen of heaven and votaress of the place;
> Only, she bowed, she stooped as she would kiss
> The ground and turn its misery into bliss—
> Even so she hovered in hell-haunted space;
> It looked that every moment she must drop,
> She and her Baby, from the jagged tower's top.

The story is easy and its whole atmosphere is created by the contrast of ordinary devotional images and the 'mad plague murderous' of devastation's 'airy devils'. When the statue falls the war will end; in God's time an end will be put to war, 'worse than a ghoul'.

'Thomasine', the earlier of the two poems, has a more involved story of a dream, and the figure of Thomasine enchants her lover and the reader; but who is this figure of youth, of life or imagination—'That call in the reeds was all her theme':

> I dare not screen
> My thought from the chance that just this one
> Reed-note from beyond the world else known
> Woke a new song in sauntering Thomasine.

Reality is suspended, Thomasine emerges as a symbol of hope in universal love; the poem ends quietly and with imaginative delicacy:

> Day and life ahead;
> Would it were mine to utter more
> Than from some broken knowledge now was said,
> And trace them in Time's wonder, shore on shore
> Achieving; only trust we this,
> Under our harsh world wells such constant bliss.

Blessed it is, and when it upsprings through,
Its beauty assails the worst that hate can do.
Blessed that sign of venture given, that chime
From solitude when reeds are green,
And answered as by Thomasine
Through the tangles of chance and time.

The poems were written during the war and the restless post-war years, and in the harsh uncertainty of that period Blunden seems to have felt a personal challenge that the artist should maintain and assert his faith in more permanent values.

Though his later poems were calmer, the power and force remained and were conditioned by his own career, rather than by any lessening of international tension which did not occur. For he returned to Japan for two years on the Foreign Office mission. After a short stay at the office of *The Times Literary Supplement*, in 1953 he accepted an invitation to become Professor of English at the University of Hong Kong. During his stay he received the award of the Queen's Gold Medal for Poetry, and to celebrate his sixty-fifth birthday local students managed to publish a volume of tributes that included a formidable list of names from many parts.

To anticipate, he retired from Hong Kong in 1964. Two years later, after a stormy campaign in which characteristically he played little part, he was elected Professor of Poetry, an appointment from which he prematurely resigned on medical advice.

So the volume *A Hong Kong House* (1962) ranged over a variety of themes; absence can sharpen memory, and thoughts of the English and French countrysides, or pictures of people, known and unknown, are sympathetically and clearly defined. However, not unnaturally, the main emphasis was derived from the east; often as in the title-poem he describes in detail—with humour—the surroundings of the natural eastern world, or, as formerly, he wanders in thought:

> Is it Meredith's Westermain, or an eastern world's
>   enchantments
> That haunt me at this hour of night? the summer sighing
>   Music and breath of the branches
>   In some strange manner pass.

The quietness is perhaps due to his thought that 'The East has all the time, the West has none.' Many of these poems have a lyrical delicacy of expression and style that suggests the quality of clear porcelain. As a mere flower or two, a bird or insect are sufficient to create the effect of a scroll painting of considerable depth and feeling, so Blunden is sparse with his images, and by observing a microcosm reflects the macrocosm of his own questionings. Watching a 'thin strange fly' on his desk, he ponders:

> . . . how this being from the world unknown
> Knew this would be *the* place
> I wondered—but it knew its own
> And came along with passionate pace

The answer provides a wider reflection:

> I chanced to unconceal
> What almost made me kneel—
> The attempted nest, the nursery of clay,
> So near our own, such mysteries away,
> So near ourselves and the chief of our little day.

In a similar vein, in the midst of 'bricks and smoke' a thrush, messenger of spring,

>   spoke
> Brave from the top of one fine walnut tree,
> From one same twig—and why that one? So he
> Looked round the compass all ways, singing loud
> Hour on bleak hour, beneath blue sky or cloud.

But the sequel differs as the walnuts ripen

>   One more year achieves
> Its central calm, dawns come and suns unclose,
> Without the music's wonder so few heard

> From that enchanted and enchanting bird,
> Flown into mystery, who perched so clear
> And sang so well to tell us spring was here.

The bird itself is 'enchanted' as though according to some great scheme, and with the fly, acts its part through the agency of a superior force. The parallel with the human condition is evident; man too might well understand more humbly his own limitations. In 'The Stone Garden in Kyoto' he is explicit:

> Let me like many others pause
> By these mysterious forms of stone,
> Which seem to speak eternal laws,
> Truths which must not become unknown
> At any point in time and space.

Such poems follow on from many of Blunden's earlier metaphysical probings. From experience he seems to accept King Lear's 'mystery of things'—and the word and idea of 'mystery' occur frequently—the recognition of or belief in 'eternal laws' extends beyond any rational explanation that the human mind can make.

X

Future literary historians attempting to evaluate the period from 1914, when Blunden published his first book of poems, to 1971 will have to sort out a confusion of differing ideas; as with the general condition of the world, so many fashions have had meteoric uprisings, only to vanish very rapidly to be replaced by other transitory luminaries. Blunden wrote in 1956:

Changes of professional judgement are so frequent... I have seen with surprise how beloved examples have become horrible examples, and how a new day blows its trumpets for writings hard to connect with what *was* poetry just before.

His poetic career began when the writing and reading of poetry was a widespread occupation—the large number of soldiers who took to composing verses in the trenches is a good example. That they did not all reach great heights does not remove the interest which prompted them. By the thirties poetry magazines were in difficulties; a wave of intellectual 'clever' obscurity tried to take over, which caused many general readers to turn elsewhere for their enjoyment. To use Dr Johnson's words 'you had to be learned to read them'. In the natural course of events 'the wheel has come full circle', and a new generation would seem to be anxious to communicate their thoughts and ideas to a wider public which is responding to their efforts.

For a while Blunden came under the cloud of being a 'Georgian'; merely to have had a poem included in any of Edward Marsh's collections (made to encourage younger poets), was a critical cause for damnation! As with many 'labels' this one has proved to be of little significance and Blunden has pursued his own course, perhaps isolated in the true artistic sense, and perhaps as a literary scholar conscious that the poet should be 'above the battle' of the moment— but not oblivious to the events of his time. C. Day Lewis wrote on Blunden's fiftieth birthday that he

> never has burned or bowed
> To popular gods, and when fame beckons
> Modestly melts in the crowd.

For too long anthologists have scarcely looked beyond a few of his early pieces, a common fault, and though these are deservedly popular they are hardly adequate to represent the scope of a poet who has been writing and publishing for over half a century.

The corpus of his work both in verse and prose is formidable and comprehensive. English literature owes much to him for his biographical discoveries, critical originality and perspicuity; literary periods are now the fuller for his researches. The Romantics, for example, apart from his considerations of central figures, have more depth of atmosphere and knowledge because of his treatment of Leigh Hunt, Kirke White, John Taylor, and, above all, of John Clare. His edition of William Collins with the prefatory biographical essay and his appreciation of many other quiet poets of the eighteenth century have enlarged the understanding of the period, and adjusted the positions of the great names. Shakespeare, the seventeenth century, with Milton, Vaughan, Traherne, and Herbert in particular, by his sympathetic and imaginative treatment, have often had 'dead' passages brought to life.

To this animated criticism belong the many verse tributes to past authors in which a portrait is painted of the spirit and mind of the subject, which only with great difficulty and less emotion could be contained in prose. His prose is closely linked to his verse; it has the same nervous accuracy and rhythm. Modesty and shrewdness are the qualities that make appropriate the temper of a Warton Lecture, and equally appear in lectures for a Japanese university. He does not 'play down' to his readers or audience; he demands their close attention, but he knows them perhaps better than they know themselves !

Another field in which he shows himself the inheritor of good literary traditions is that of ceremonial or occasional verses. Such pieces have for long been the amusement of poets. The 'occasional' poet has to be able to write for the moment, to unite craftsmanship with a touch of personality to sympathetic propriety. Blunden has provided a profusion of such moments and given his own standard whether writing verses on the death of King George V or a madrigal for the Queen's Coronation, a birthday greeting, a prologue to a play or a compliment to the citizens of a Japanese town.

On a more serious plane his poetic range has been extensively varied. It was as a poet of the countryside that he acquired his early reputation. Returning from the devastation of the French countryside, he appreciated more deeply the apparently undisturbed peace of Kent and East Anglia;

the early poems cover a wide area of experience and observation in which landscape, tree or stream not only reveal their natural essential beauty but have a larger connexion with man and his world. These are not poems of nostalgia, but they often have a poignancy which indicates that despite the quietness the world of 1919 was changing, and several sinister notes were heard to suggest that the ways of nature were no longer as mild as formerly. They were almost valedictions to his own youth, but in many respects he can be considered as a 'nature-poet' in the Wordsworthian sense. He never fills in all the scene; the detail is minute, but something more could be told. His experience across the world, while finding similar ideas of feeling, makes it impossible to believe that his imaginative conception is confined to any one local area.

With all other personal experiences, the years spent in the trenches have never ceased to influence him in a variety of intellectual and emotional senses. At the time he was younger than most of the other recognized 'war-poets', his life had been more restricted, being spent in the village schoolmaster's house or in the somewhat cloistered atmosphere of Christ's Hospital, and he spent more time in and around the trenches than most of the contemporary writers. He has said that he did not publish many war-poems in his early collections because the reading public was tired of war and war-writers. But in *The Waggoner* appeared one of the finest war-poems, 'Third Ypres', which in its intensity and understated horror reveals the scarring impact of war on individuals. It was typical of Blunden's war-poems; he makes an indictment against war through a personal exposure rather than indulging in invective. In a hundred and thirty lines he covers three days and two nights; time was meaningless:

Each moment puffed into a year with death.

The poem explores the isolation of the soldier unaware of what is happening around him; so the subjective movement is from blithe optimism to 'the abyss of madness'.

Much has been written about the appearance of so many
war-poets of the period; no really satisfying explanation has
been given, but the usual impression is that once the war
was over, so was the crippling mental effect. To some extent
this was true; while many such as Wilfred Owen were
killed, others wrote their experiences 'out of their systems'
with memoirs or retrospective general attacks. Blunden
absorbed all his into his temperament, which clearly have
become part of the poet. This is shown not only in regular
tributes to individuals, or to memories of single episodes,
but more indirectly and unexpectedly, and no collection is
without some reference to war moments.

This may account for some of his isolation as a poet,
living in a timeless world where past and present are often
indistinct, and as he looks happily on the flourishing fields
around the river Ancre, the other aspect of a nature
destroyed can recur to his mind. A fearfulness that the
'balance of nature' is so often lightly poised suggests that
man is not always welcome:

> I am for the woods against the world,
> But are the woods for me?

In his metaphysical moments the idea that 'This is God's
curious proving' has led him into considerable speculation.
In a recent poem 'A Swan, A Man' he delicately amalga-
mates several of his visionary thoughts of the man 'who
loveth well / Both man and bird and beast':

> Among the dead reeds, the single swan
> Floats and explores the water-shallow under,
> While the wet whistling wind blows on
> And the path by the river is all alone,
> And I at the old bridge wonder
> If those are birds or leaves,
> Small quick birds or withered leaves,
> Astir on the grassy patch of green
> Where the wind is not so rough and keen.

What happens to my thought-time,
To my desires, my deeds, this day?
The rainstorm beats the pitiful stream
With battle-pictures I had hoped to miss,
But winter warfare could be worse than this;
Into the house, recall what dead friends say,
And like the Ancient Mariner learn to pray.

Much of the truth that he realized through his wide
knowledge of literary traditions together with his sharp
awareness of the implications of his own experience has now
become evident; he is often more 'contemporary' in thought
than is sometimes realized. In an age of noise, the quality of
the 'unheard' or 'unspoken' essence of true poetry is not
easily caught. His artistic sincerity and modesty are part of
his inheritance. His faith in poetry has a long classical
authority:

The principal thing is still with me; poetry is as much a part of the
universe as mathematics and physics. It is not a clever device or recrea-
tion, unless the Eternal is clever. Many are conscious of it as experience,
though, as Hardy hints, sometimes when it was most at hand 'we were
looking away'. In various modes of speech and impressions of metre
many seek to do justice to this quality in human life. Music may have
the advantage, and painting—for certain times. The method of language
of conveying some perception of the grace beyond the facts is open to
all: for me the essence of the blessing is often given in some melody and
sidelight by an 'unimportant' poet where I find the great ones marching
on another objective after all.

EDMUND BLUNDEN

A Select Bibliography

(Place of publication London, unless stated otherwise)

Bibliography:

A BIBLIOGRAPHY OF EDMUND BLUNDEN, by B. J. Kirkpatrick (in preparation).

Collections:

POEMS (1930).

POEMS, 1930–1940 (1940).

EDMUND BLUNDEN: A SELECTION OF HIS POETRY AND PROSE; ed. K. Hopkins (1950).

POEMS OF MANY YEARS (1957)
—includes poems hitherto unpublished.

Separate Works. Verse:

POEMS; Horsham (1914).

POEMS TRANSLATED FROM THE FRENCH; Horsham (1914).

THREE POEMS; Uckfield (1916).

THE BARN, WITH CERTAIN OTHER POEMS; Uckfield (1916)
—the two Uckfield publications were also issued as one volume, *The Harbingers*, 1916.

PASTORALS: A Book of Verses (1916).

THE WAGGONER, AND OTHER POEMS (1920).

THE SHEPHERD, AND OTHER POEMS OF PEACE AND WAR (1922).

OLD HOMES: A Poem; Clare (1922).

ENGLISH POEMS (1925).

RETREAT (1928).

NEAR AND FAR: New Poems (1929).

THE WEATHERCOCK—LA GIROUETTE, 1917 (1931).

HALFWAY HOUSE: A Miscellany (1932).

CHOICE OR CHANCE (1934)
—limited edition.

AN ELEGY, AND OTHER POEMS (1937).

ON SEVERAL OCCASIONS (1938)
—limited edition.

39

SHELLS BY A STREAM (1944).

AFTER THE BOMBING, AND OTHER SHORT POEMS (1949).

THE DEDE OF PITTIE: Dramatic scenes reflecting the history of Christ's
   Hospital and offered in celebration of the quatercentenary (1953).
   Verse and Prose

A HONG KONG HOUSE: Poems 1951-1961 (1962)

—the title poem was separately published, London 1959.

ELEVEN POEMS; Cambridge (1965)

—limited edition.

THE MIDNIGHT SKATERS: Poems for young readers, ed. C. Day Lewis
   (1968).

Separate Works. Prose:

THE BONADVENTURE: A random journal of an Atlantic holiday (1922)

CHRIST'S HOSPITAL: A retrospect [1923].

ON THE POEMS OF HENRY VAUGHAN: Characteristics and imitations
   (1927).

UNDERTONES OF WAR (1928)

—with a Supplement of Poetical Interpretations and Variations. The
   World's Classics edition, 1956, has a new preface. New edition,
   1965.

LEIGH HUNT'S 'EXAMINER' EXAMINED (1928)

—reprinted with a new preface, 1967.

NATURE IN ENGLISH LITERATURE (1929).

LEIGH HUNT: A biography (1930).

DE BELLO GERMANICO: A fragment of trench history; Hawstead (1930).

VOTIVE TABLETS: Studies chiefly appreciative of English authors and
   books (1931).

THE FACE OF ENGLAND, IN A SERIES OF OCCASIONAL SKETCHES (1932).
   Prose and Verse.

WE'LL SHIFT OUR GROUND, OR, TWO ON A TOUR: ALMOST A NOVEL (1933)

—in collaboration with Sylva Norman.

CHARLES LAMB AND HIS CONTEMPORARIES; Cambridge (1933)

—the Clark Lectures, delivered at Trinity College, Cambridge, 1932.

THE MIND'S EYE: Essays (1934).

KEATS'S PUBLISHER: A memoir of John Taylor, 1781-1864 (1936).

ENGLISH VILLAGES (1941)

—in the 'Britain in Pictures' Series.

THOMAS HARDY (1941)

—in the 'English Men of Letters' Series.

ROMANTIC POETRY AND THE FINE ARTS (1942)
—the Warton Lecture on English Poetry delivered before the British Academy, 1942.

CRICKET COUNTRY (1944).

SHELLEY: A life story (1946).

SHAKESPEARE TO HARDY: Short studies of characteristic English authors; Tokyo (1948).

ADDRESSES ON GENERAL SUBJECTS CONNECTED WITH ENGLISH LITERATURE; Tokyo (1949).

SONS OF LIGHT: A series of lectures on English writers; Tokyo (1949).

POETRY AND SCIENCE, AND OTHER LECTURES; Osaka (1949).

FAVOURITE STUDIES IN ENGLISH LITERATURE: Lectures given at Keio University; Tokyo (1950).

INFLUENTIAL BOOKS: Lectures given at Waseda University; Tokyo [1950].

REPRINTED PAPERS: Partly concerning some English romantic poets; Tokyo (1950).

JOHN KEATS (1950)
—in 'Writers and their Work' Series. Revised editions, 1954, 1959, 1966.

CHAUCER TO 'B.V.'; Tokyo (1950)
—'B.V.' is the poet James Thomson, 1834-82.

A WANDERER IN JAPAN; Tokyo [1950].

CHARLES LAMB (1954)
—in 'Writers and their Work' Series. Revised edition, 1964.

WAR POETS, 1914-1918 (1958)
—in 'Writers and their Work' series.

A WESSEX WORTHY: Thomas Russell; Beaminster (1960).

ENGLISH SCIENTISTS AS MEN OF LETTERS (1961)
—Jubilee Congress lecture delivered 11 September 1961, University of Hong Kong.

LEE LAN FLIES THE DRAGON KITE, by R. Herrmans (1962). *Translation*

WILLIAM CROWE, 1745-1829; Beaminster (1963).

EDWARDIAN ENGLAND, 1901-1914, ed. S. Nowell-Smith (1964)
—contains an essay 'County Childhood', by Edmund Blunden.

GUEST OF THOMAS HARDY; Beaminster (1964)
—monographs on the life of Thomas Hardy. No. 10.

A BRIEF GUIDE TO THE GREAT CHURCH OF THE HOLY TRINITY, LONG MELFORD; Long Melford (1965)
—new edition 1966.

A FEW NOT QUITE FORGOTTEN WRITERS? (1967)
—English Association Presidential Address, 1967.
PROMISE OF GREATNESS: The War of 1914-1918, ed. G. A. Parnichas
   (1968)
—contains an essay by Blunden 'Infantryman passes by'.

Works Edited or Compiled:

JOHN CLARE: Poems, chiefly from manuscript (1920)
—in collaboration with Alan Porter.
MADRIGALS AND CHRONICLES: Being newly found poems written by
   John Clare (1924).
A SONG TO DAVID, BY CHRISTOPHER SMART (1924).
THE ORIENTAL LITERARY TIMES (1925-   ).
SHELLEY AND KEATS, AS THEY STRUCK THEIR CONTEMPORARIES (1925).
A HUNDRED ENGLISH POEMS; Tokyo (1927).
—new and revised edition, 1949.
THE POEMS OF WILLIAM COLLINS (1929).
SKETCHES IN THE LIFE OF JOHN CLARE WRITTEN BY HIMSELF (1931).
THE POEMS OF WILFRED OWEN (1931).
CHARLES LAMB: His life recorded by his contemporaries (1934).
HYMNS FOR THE AMUSEMENT OF CHILDREN, BY CHRISTOPHER SMART;
   Oxford (1947)
—printed for the Luttrell Society.
THE LIFE OF GEORGE CRABBE, by his son. With an introduction by
   E. Blunden.
SHELLEY'S DEFENCE OF POETRY; Tokyo (1948).
THE CHRIST'S HOSPITAL BOOK (1953)
—in collaboration with E. Bennett, P. Y. Carter and J. E. Morpurgo.
POEMS BY IVOR GURNEY (1954).
SELECTED POEMS: SHELLEY (1954).
SELECTED POEMS: J. KEATS (1955).
SELECTED POEMS OF TENNYSON (1960).
WAYSIDE POEMS OF THE SEVENTEENTH CENTURY: An anthology;
   Hong Kong (1963)
—in collaboration with B. Mellor.
WAYSIDE POEMS OF THE EARLY EIGHTEENTH CENTURY: An anthology;
   Hong Kong (1964).
THE SOLITARY SONG: Poems for young readers, by William Words-
   worth (1970).

Some Critical Studies:

THE DIALECTAL WORDS IN BLUNDEN'S POEMS, by Robert Bridges; Oxford (1921)
—Tract No. V of the Society for Pure English.

AN ANATOMY OF POETRY, by A. Williams-Ellis; Oxford (1922).

ESSAYS ON POETRY, by J. C. Squire (1923).

MOVEMENTS IN MODERN ENGLISH POETRY AND PROSE, by W. Sherard Vines; Tokyo (1927).

EDMUND BLUNDEN, HIS PROFESSORSHIP AND HIS WRITINGS; Tokyo (1927).

NEW PATHS ON HELICON, by Henry Newbolt (1927).

SUNDAY MORNINGS, by J. C. Squire (1930)
—articles from *The Observer.*

POETRY AT PRESENT, by C. W. S. Williams; Oxford (1930).

FROM SURTEES TO SASSOON: Some English contrasts 1838-1928, by F. J. Harvey Darton (1931).

SECOND IMPRESSIONS, by T. Earle Welby (1933).

AUTHORS TODAY AND YESTERDAY, by S. J. Kunitz; New York (1933).

MODERN ENGLISH POETRY, 1882-1932, by R. L. Mégroz (1933).

EIGHT FOR IMMORTALITY, by Richard Church (1941).

REFLECTIONS IN A MIRROR: second series, by Charles Morgan (1946).

POETS AND PUNDITS: Essays and addresses, by H. l'A. Fausset (1947).

COLLECTED POEMS, by C. Day Lewis (1954)
—includes 'Lines for Edmund Blunden on his Fiftieth Birthday', p.282.

TALKING OF BOOKS, by Oliver Edwards (1957).

EDMUND BLUNDEN, SIXTY FIVE, ed. Chau Wah Ching, and others; by various authors; Hong Kong (1961).

Acknowledgment: The quotations from Mr Blunden's work in this essay appear with his kind permission and that of Messrs Collins, who published *Poems of Many Years.*

WRITERS AND THEIR WORK

General Surveys:
THE DETECTIVE STORY IN BRITAIN: Julian Symons
THE ENGLISH BIBLE: Donald Coggan
ENGLISH VERSE EPIGRAM: G. Rostrevor Hamilton
ENGLISH HYMNS: A. Pollard
ENGLISH MARITIME WRITING: Hakluyt to Cook: Oliver Warner
THE ENGLISH SHORT STORY I: & II: T. O. Beachcroft
THE ENGLISH SONNET: P. Cruttwell
ENGLISH SERMONS: Arthur Pollard
ENGLISH TRANSLATORS and TRANSLATIONS: J. M. Cohen
ENGLISH TRAVELLERS IN THE NEAR EAST: Robin Fedden
THREE WOMEN DIARISTS: M. Willy

Sixteenth Century and Earlier:
FRANCIS BACON: J. Max Patrick
BEAUMONT & FLETCHER: Ian Fletcher
CHAUCER: Nevill Coghill
GOWER & LYDGATE: Derek Pearsall
RICHARD HOOKER: A. Pollard
THOMAS KYD: Philip Edwards
LANGLAND: Nevill Coghill
LYLY & PEELE: G. K. Hunter
MALORY: M. C. Bradbrook
MARLOWE: Philip Henderson
SIR THOMAS MORE: E. E. Reynolds
RALEGH: Agnes Latham
SIDNEY: Kenneth Muir
SKELTON: Peter Green
SPENSER: Rosemary Freeman
THREE 14TH-CENTURY ENGLISH MYSTICS: Phyllis Hodgson
TWO SCOTS CHAUCERIANS: H. Harvey Wood
WYATT: Sergio Baldi

Seventeenth Century:
SIR THOMAS BROWNE: Peter Green
BUNYAN: Henri Talon
CAVALIER POETS: Robin Skelton
CONGREVE: Bonamy Dobrée
DONNE: F. Kermode
DRYDEN: Bonamy Dobrée
ENGLISH DIARISTS: Evelyn and Pepys: M. Willy
FARQUHAR: A. J. Farmer
JOHN FORD: Clifford Leech
GEORGE HERBERT: T. S. Eliot
HERRICK: John Press
HOBBES: T. E. Jessop
BEN JONSON: J. B. Bamborough

LOCKE: Maurice Cranston
ANDREW MARVELL: John Press
MILTON: E. M. W. Tillyard
RESTORATION COURT POETS: V. de S. Pinto
SHAKESPEARE: C. J. Sisson
CHRONICLES: Clifford Leech
EARLY COMEDIES: Derek Traversi
LATER COMEDIES: G. K. Hunter
FINAL PLAYS: F. Kermode
HISTORIES: L. C. Knights
POEMS: F. T. Prince
PROBLEM PLAYS: Peter Ure
ROMAN PLAYS: T. J. B. Spencer
GREAT TRAGEDIES: Kenneth Muir
THREE METAPHYSICAL POETS: Margaret Willy
WEBSTER: Ian Scott-Kilvert
WYCHERLEY: P. F. Vernon

Eighteenth Century:
BERKELEY: T. E. Jessop
BLAKE: Kathleen Raine
BOSWELL: P. A. W. Collins
BURKE: T. E. Utley
BURNS: David Daiches
WM. COLLINS: Oswald Doughty
COWPER: N. Nicholson
CRABBE: R. L. Brett
DEFOE: J. R. Sutherland
FIELDING: John Butt
GAY: Oliver Warner
GIBBON: C. V. Wedgwood
GOLDSMITH: A. Norman Jeffares
GRAY: R. W. Ketton-Cremer
HUME: Montgomery Belgion
SAMUEL JOHNSON: S. C. Roberts
POPE: Ian Jack
RICHARDSON: R. F. Brissenden
SHERIDAN: W. A. Darlington
CHRISTOPHER SMART: G. Grigson
SMOLLETT: Laurence Brander
STEELE, ADDISON: A. R. Humphreys
STERNE: D. W. Jefferson
SWIFT: J. Middleton Murry
SIR JOHN VANBRUGH: Bernard Harris
HORACE WALPOLE: Hugh Honour

Nineteenth Century:
MATTHEW ARNOLD: Kenneth Allott
JANE AUSTEN: S. Townsend Warner
BAGEHOT: N. St John-Stevas
BRONTË SISTERS: Phyllis Bentley
BROWNING: John Bryson
E. B. BROWNING: Alethea Hayter
SAMUEL BUTLER: G. D. H. Cole
BYRON: Bernard Blackstone